Praise for The Clearing Process...

I have been a student of metaphysics and New Thought for over 25 years. Recently I experienced a particularly challenging emotional situation in which all my years of spiritual practice confused me. Pat was gently able to guide me back to my spiritual foundation by leading me to go deeper into the mystery, and allowing my inner guidance to resurface. Her wisdom and the Clearing Process are a life raft for me.

Rita McLain, Forest Knolls, CA

Rev. Pat Palmer has written a powerful book that anyone can use to clear out emotional wounds. The Clearing Process is a step by step process that enables one to feel and then release toxic emotions. The result of using the process is freedom and renewed sources of energy and joy.

Nevin Valentine
Certified Relationship Coach; Imago Couples International

I LOVED your book Pat! It is very clear and easy to follow and I KNOW how powerful this kind of work is. I am going to recommend it to my spiritual group!

Rev. Grace Koch

"The Clearing Process is one of the best techniques I know of for unearthing and releasing those old emotions and belief systems we unconsciously hold which create lifelong patterns affecting every aspect of our being."

Lisa Pasquinelli, Ph.D.
Clinical Psychologist, San Rafael, CA

This book is incredible - it's like GOLD!! Such straight forward help! The writing is very clear -- and makes sense. I'm really impressed with the structure and order of it. There are people out there who are really READY to do this work, and this book will be their Bible. You and your Soul wrote this book!

Carina Reisberg, Rife Therapist

The Clearing Process Workbook

Rev. Pat M. Palmer

The Clearing Process Workbook is written by Rev. Pat Palmer to accompany the original guidebook, "The Clearing Process...for Conscious Living."

Further information is available at the website www.clearingprocess.com.

Pat Palmer may be contacted at clearingprocess@icloud.com to arrange for personal counseling either in person, or via computer.

ISBN: 978 -1-300 - 38705 - 3.

No part of this book may be used or reproduced in any manner whatsoever without the written permission of the Publisher. Printed in the United States of America.

Cataloging Publication Data

1. Self-Help   2. Spiritual   3. Transformation   4. Healing

Dedication

This workbook is dedicated to all the brave self-explorers who read the
original guidebook "The Clearing Process…for Conscious Living"
and have used the process to find empowerment and freedom.

By owning and being with your deepest feelings as they occur,
you open the door to your own highest potential and greatest joy.
You are consciously on the path of who you
entered this journey to be!

I honor you for your vision, your willingness, and your courage.

Contents

Section I - The Power of the Clearing Process   Page 9

Introduction   Page 11

Beginning to See   Page 13

Your Story   Page 15

Your Greater Story   Page 19

Clearing - A Surprising Process   Page 24

Spiritual Awareness   Page 28

The Hidden Abuse   Page 32

The Underlying Philosophy   Page 35

The Childhood Phase   Page 39

Pave the Way for Your Healing   Page 42

Section II - The Six-Step Clearing Process   Page 43

Step 1: Awareness and Acceptance   Page 45
Step 2: Name it Precisely   Page 51
Step 3: When Before   Page 56
Step 4: Own Your Life   Page 61
Step 5: Being With   Page 65
Step 6: Lighten Up   Page 76

Clearing Process Worksheet   Page 79

Let the Light Continue to Shine   Page 81

SECTION I

The Power of the Clearing Process

There are many ways to experience life. Our physical, mental and emotional bodies are perfectly equipped to live it powerfully, as conduits of the spiritual energy that creates things by becoming them.

However, we cannot respond to life situations from our now-perspective, if we are fogged by negative energies we don't even realize we are carrying. Moreover, when we are holding them, we unknowingly create circumstances that continue to call those energies forth. We are meant to be live in freedom. If the heart is congested with old pain; e.g. fear, anger, sadness, we cannot be free.

Section I of this Workbook prepares one for easily and effectively clearing. The Clearing Process is a straight forward, easily-followed method for releasing energies we no longer want or need to hold. We become clear and light, able to more fully connect with our divine Self.

We are created as purely vibrational beings. When we transform and uplift our own frequency, we serve humanity as a clearer element of itself. We heal not only our own life, but that of the world.

Introduction

I sometimes confess to people, "I don't LIKE this Clearing Process!!" And that is a true statement. It's not much fun to make myself go deeply into my feelings - feelings that I don't want to even have in the first place!

And then on top of that, the process also requires remembering myself in childhood situations that I didn't invite! I find myself reluctant to even set aside the time to do that.

And yet, this is by far the most effective transformative process I have yet encountered. Not only does it dissolve my unwanted feelings; it amazingly results in shifts in the behavior of people in my life - people I previously worked on changing, to no avail. In other words, as I heal, my vibration shifts; therefore life responds differently to me.

In short, it's not necessary to like the Clearing Process, only to do it! Hence this Workbook.

After writing the guidebook, "The Clearing Process...for Conscious Living" I began to receive feedback from readers and from current and former clients. They helped me realize that while the process gradually becomes a powerful self-therapy when one uses it, we really need to have assistance in the beginning.

For one thing, it is challenging to stay with it; we can be too easily distracted when we're not even sure that an uncomfortable process is going to produce results. Another deterrent is the difficulty of making oneself enter into and stay with painful emotions. It is much easier to try to figure out why something is happening, and what to do about the situation, than to feel it!

This Workbook is written to provide you with invaluable stepping stones to success in clearing those old issues that are still running your life. It is a surrogate therapist.

First read the guidebook, to understand the rationale and the intentions of the process, and to develop a willingness to delve into your own deep self. Then take your time in doing the exercises provided here. This is the kind of activity in which going slowly provides a huge pay-off.

Now…may you be filled with the expectation of transformation! First you will experience greater ease in your relationships - beginning with your own relationship with self.

As you build faith in your ability to accept and be with your own feelings, you will carry a quiet joy, even while in the throes of something you want to clear up in your life.

Gradually you will develop familiarity with this tool for personal growth, and get into the excitement of witnessing your own evolution! That's what this Life journey is really all about.

Beginning to See

This Clearing Process Workbook is written to accompany "The Clearing Process …for Conscious Living" guidebook. It is important that you first have read the guidebook and that you have it handy, as you complete these exercises. This is not meant to be an independent workbook, although it can be used that way, if you don't have access to the text.

Use the workbook exercises in the order in which they occur. It would be best not to skip anything, as the results are generated by the cumulative effect. You will find topics in approximately the same order as presented in the book. All of the assignments involve you interacting with your self. You know yourself better than anyone else does. Deep inquiry and honest answers to the questions will provide more information and guidance for you than anything you hear from other sources.

Toward this end, please create a journal if you don't already have one - not a journal for recording your activities; keep it only for inner insights and experiences. Writing is an important technique for unfolding awareness. Saying whatever you want without holding back, like you can in a journal, becomes a catalyst for the release of emotions.

Many responses to the workbook exercises will be longer than the space provided for them, and your journal is the best place to do additional writing, rather than shortening your responses.

While the actual Clearing Process itself consists of only six steps, in preparation for doing this work it is important to develop an alignment with the underlying philosophy. The core principle is that any difficult situations we have in our life today are bringing up exactly the same emotions that we had, but could not process, in our early life.

In my opinion, the phrase "the truth shall set you free" refers to this very phenomenon. The 'truth' is that as little children our primary mandate was to love our parents; therefore anything that we felt which was not loving had to be squashed, at least until we were older. It's also true that in many families it was not permissible to feel certain feelings. Therefore we repressed not only those emotions, but even the knowledge that we <u>had</u> those feelings.

Now, through turning toward the depth of our present-time emotions, we are finally able to experience the truth about the inner experiences of our very young years. Because they are replicating themselves in our life now, we get to see what we can't even remember! (That is one of the miracles of life - how that amazing process supports our inner evolution.)

When we feel the emotions - unlike we could when young - the energy holding them in place releases. They were just waiting to be recognized! We become 'free' because that toxic energy, which has been held in every cell in our body, is no longer drawing people and situations to us to bring up the old emotions to be seen.

We begin creating life from the choice for joy and success, rather than from inadvertently needing to heal the past. Our vibration is different, with the toxic feelings clearing and repressive energy freed up! People change their attitudes and behavior toward us without even realizing it. Our attention focuses on different things.

We are beginning to see....

Your Story

What was your childhood like? What situations occurred which might have caused you to have emotions that you were not able to consciously feel or express? We still carry the vibrations of whatever psychic energy was not able to move freely through us as children. It radiates out from us subliminally, greatly affecting our present life.

♥ Personal Reflections...

...Write a brief autobiography, describing your young childhood, with the issues that your mom, dad or other significant caregivers had, and how they affected you.

_____

_____

_____

_____

_____

_____

_____

_____

_____

_____

_____

_____

_____

_____

_____

...How have you worked on releasing and transforming toxic energy that you carried into your adult life; *e.g. therapy, classes, spiritual pursuits?*

_____

_____

_____

_____

_____

_____

_____

_____

_____

_____

_____

_____

_____

_____

_____

_____

...How do you handle challenging situations that come up in your life today?

_____

_____

_____

Your Greater Story

This life is part of the journey of our soul. We are born with an agenda, choosing to come into this human incarnation on earth for specific purposes, not so much to accomplish something on the physical plane, but rather to transform energies we are carrying in our eternal self.

The people, places and things we draw to ourselves are all in reflection of that journey; our props along the way. Even the root family and circumstances of our childhood were chosen by our soul to facilitate this unique purpose.

♥_Personal Reflections..._

...What abilities and positive personality characteristics were developed in you as a result of your childhood family?

_____

_____

_____

_____

_____

_____

_____

_____

_____

_____

_____

_____

_____

_____

_____

_____

_____

_____

_____

_____

_____

…What is your sense of life purpose as it has developed
through using those parts of your self?

_____

_____

_____

_____

_____

_____

_____

_____

_____

_____

_____

_____

_____

_____

_____

_____

_____

_____

…Are there inabilities or frustrations that you realize you still carry as a result of dysfunctional parenting or influences on you as a child?

_____

_____

_____

_____

_____

_____

_____

_____

_____

...How have they affected your life journey?

_____

_____

_____

_____

_____

_____

_____

_____

_____

_____

...Are there emotions that you find yourself holding
repeatedly in your life? Identify some of the circumstances
that seem to bring them up.

_____

_____

_____

_____

_____

_____

Clearing - A Surprising Process

Most approaches to dealing with problem issues focus on understanding Why something is happening to a person, and what things one might Do to make changes in the situation. The Clearing Process is unique in that we don't ask either of those questions.

The Why

♥ Personal Reflections...

...Consider the last emotional challenge you encountered in your life. Describe it briefly, including Why you think it happened to you.

_____

_____

_____

_____

_____

_____

_____

_____

_____

_____

_____

_____

_____

_____

Actually, focusing on the Why can be a deterrent to healing. Too often, even therapists settle for talking through and understanding personal traumas and dramas as an adequate pathway to change. It feels so rewarding to have insights and to understand at last!

Actually, understanding can be the 'booby prize!'

The real reason WHY negative outcomes repeat in our experience is because we unknowingly draw them to us through the choices we make. We are inadvertently led to create situations that will bring up in us the feelings we've been unconsciously holding all of our adult lives. We keep given ourselves another opportunity to heal them.

That is the only real answer to Why certain feelings/things happen to us over and over again.

The What to Do

When we have a situation that is disturbing, our first recourse is usually to determine what to DO to make it better.

♥ Personal Reflections...

...In the situation you described above, what did you try to Do to transform it; to change the other person's or your own behavior, and to feel better?

_____

_____

_____

_____

_____

_____

_____

_____

_____

_____

_____

_____

_____

Wondering what to DO about the negative experiences usually means trying to change our own or another's behavior. We are trying to change the one situation. What is really wanted however, is permanent change.

True healing comes from feeling the intense emotion that comes up - without blaming the person who seems to be causing it. That approach is what will dissolve it forever. Loving attention to the woundedness is what heals.

Forgiveness

Forgiveness is another frequently sought pathway to healing. We try to forgive others for the things they did to cause us pain. Many times well-intentioned others, who want to help us, encourage forgiveness as the only course of action.

♥ _Personal Reflections..._

...Describe a situation in which you felt wronged, and tried to forgive. How successful have you been in this effort? Has it transformed?

_____

_____

_____

_____

_____

_____

_____

_____

_____

_____

_____

_____

_____

_____

_____

_____

_____

_____

_____

_____

Forgiveness, like understanding, can feel good; however it does not help dissipate unconscious negative vibration we are holding. We can forgive with our mind and heart, but the pain still needs to be dissolved, and that only happens with attention to it.

Forgiveness will come by itself, naturally, after the truth about the pain has been felt.

The temptations to dwell in figuring out WHY, the what to DO, and Forgiving, are ways that the ego keeps us busy and defends against the 'forbidden' truth-telling about how we felt/feel.

Spiritual Awareness

What we believe about how life works will greatly affect our expectations, which in turn greatly influence where we place our energy/efforts.

For example, if you believe that what you see is what you get, you will place great premium on how things appear to be. If you believe in a God who might help you, you may place emphasis on the power of prayer. If you believe in a judgmental power, you may be invested in being a good person.

♥ Personal Reflections...

...Do you have a sense of a spiritual power in your life? Describe your understanding of it; what you believe about it.

_____

_____

_____

_____

_____

_____

_____

_____

_____

_____

_____

_____

_____

_____

_____

_____

The Clearing Process is based on the spiritual dimension as fundamental to the life journey. It is not that a Spiritual Being does things to us, but rather that the process of life itself is spiritual in nature.

For one thing, each one of us is a center in the mind of spirit, and our energy vibration draws to us whatever will support our spiritual evolution. If what arrives is painful, it is because in some way we are to use this experience to move into greater joy and success in our soul's development.

♥ Personal Reflections...

...Have you had any painful experiences that you later realized were of great benefit to you?

_____

_____

_____

_____

_____

_____

_____

_____

_____

_____

_____

_____

_____

_____

_____

_____

_____

_____

_____

…Can you think of some times in which you now realize you were participating in bringing the very thing you did not want into your life?

_____

_____

_____

_____

_____

_____

_____

_____

_____

_____

…Have you ever felt like someone 'made' you feel something painful ("He makes me SO mad!") and later realized that you have felt that way <u>many</u> times in your life, with other people and in other situations?

_____

_____

_____

_____

_____

_____

_____

_____

_____

_____

_____

The Hidden Abuse

We often think of abuse as something that happens to other people, or as only referring to physical punishment. In truth, emotional abuse can be even more debilitating in its effects than some kinds of physical punishment.

Studies have shown that most people do not even realize the extent of the damage inflicted on them. Even as adults, we tend to justify our parents' sometimes negative treatment of us as deserved, and as 'not that bad.'

The problem with this whitewashing is that it keeps us from telling the truth about how much it hurt. Consequently, we are unable to attend to and dissolve the feelings.

♥ Personal Reflections...

...Do you think there were any feelings that you could not
let yourself experience as a child, but that there was reason
to feel in your family?

_____

_____

_____

_____

_____

_____

_____

_____

_____

_____

_____

_____

_____

_____

_____

_____

_____

_____

…Do you see any examples in your life today of how you intensely have this same emotion with some people close to you?

_____

_____

_____

_____

_____

_____

_____

_____

_____

_____

_____

_____

_____

_____

_____

_____

...If you were to openly express this emotion, with those you love,
how would it affect your life?

_____

_____

_____

_____

_____

_____

_____

_____

_____

The Underlying Philosophy

As you begin to use the Clearing Process, it will be more effective for you if you deeply resonate with its principles about your own evolution during this life journey.

It's not that we need to have spiritual understanding in order to live emotionally healthy lives. However, one does need to have a sense of the all-pervasiveness of Spirit, and Its action in our lives as the process of consciousness creating. Otherwise, it is impossible to believe that inner changes could so powerfully transform the things that others do and the events that happen to us.

For each of the following underlying principles of the Clearing Process, consider to what extent - from 1 (totally disagree) to 10 (fully agree) - you are comfortable with it, and circle that number.

1. Life is Perfect.   1 2 3 4 5 6 7 8 9 10

2. Spirit lives as me and is supportive to the extent I turn toward it.
                                                       1 2 3 4 5 6 7 8 9 10

3. My Soul Self chose my root family to foster in me the challenges needed to evolve.   1 2 3 4 5 6 7 8 9 10

4. Emotions I could not feel as a child, I may still carry in me in a repressed state.
                                                       1 2 3 4 5 6 7 8 9 10

5. The present is coming from the past, if the emotional intensity is greater than would be expected by the circumstance.   1 2 3 4 5 6 7 8 9 10

6. Understanding the wounding is not enough to heal it; deep feeling must occur.
                                                       1 2 3 4 5 6 7 8 9 10

7. To heal my past, I am drawn to situations that will cause those same emotions.
                                                       1 2 3 4 5 6 7 8 9 10

8. Blaming or trying to change people or circumstance does not heal the wounds.
                                                       1 2 3 4 5 6 7 8 9 10

9. Only attending to those emotions will allow them to dissipate.

1 2 3 4 5 6 7 8 9 10

10. I can't TRY to make my subconscious remember. I must invite it to reveal itself.

1 2 3 4 5 6 7 8 9 10

11. By gently encouraging myself, I will begin to remember the pain of the past.

1 2 3 4 5 6 7 8 9 10

12. I don't need to confront the person who seems to be cause; this work is with me.

1 2 3 4 5 6 7 8 9 10

13. The Clearing Process is not about forgiving!

1 2 3 4 5 6 7 8 9 10

14. I already know what to do; I just have not been able to access that knowledge.

1 2 3 4 5 6 7 8 9 10

15. The circumstances of my life will change of their own accord when I have healed.

1 2 3 4 5 6 7 8 9 10

♥ Personal Reflections...

...Notice any of the above principles with which you significantly disagree. What are your thoughts about these principles?

_____

_____

_____

_____

_____

_____

For each principle which bothers you, read more about it in Chapter 7 of the guidebook "The Clearing Process…for Conscious Living." You may also want to discuss these ideas with others in your spiritual community, and do some additional reading in some of the source books mentioned in Chapter 6.

These principles are important and worth investigating further, if you intend to seriously move ahead with this personal growth work on your own behalf. Additional discussion is also available through contacting the author, Rev. Pat Palmer at clearingprocess@icloud.com.

The Childhood Phase

The primary reason that we repress some feelings into the subconscious when we are children is for our own survival! When very young, it is critical that we believe our parents are alright, and that they love us and can take care of us. Any feeling that would call that into question must be denied and buried.

❤ Personal Reflections...

...Can you imagine any situations in your own childhood that could have created emotions you might have had to deny and not let yourself realize?

_____

_____

_____

_____

_____

_____

_____

_____

_____

_____

_____

_____

_____

_____

_____

_____

If a child has an empathetic adult to listen, such repression would not have to occur. If we did not, we cannot even trust our memory because we were not validated.

> …Was there anyone to support you by acknowledging what was happening to you?

It would seem like those old feelings repressed in childhood would lessen in intensity over the years, as we become adults. However, that is not the case. They come up, when we inadvertently invite them, with the same intensity as when they were first encountered and driven underground.

> …Have you ever witnessed yourself becoming more upset about something than the situation would warrant? (If so, very likely an old feeling from the past was being re-ignited in all its intensity.) Describe that situation, especially if it happened to you repeatedly.

_____

_____

_____

_____

_____

_____

_____

_____

_____

_____

Each of us is the best person to serve as advocate for the inner child still alive in us. We were there, and now we have the strength to tell the truth about it, along with having compassion for what that child still in us suffered.

As adults, we are able to survive knowing the truth about this, and to handle imagining and remembering how we might have felt, although it may still be painful.

Can you believe that inside of you is your childhood self, with all of your memories intact, and with any emotions that could not be felt also still intact?

    …Whisper to that inner child that now you are here to listen.
    …How does that feel?

_____

_____

_____

_____

_____

_____

Pave the way for your healing

You can talk with your own ego and assure it that it can relax. Tell it that it does not have to stay on the job of keeping those old feelings repressed.

Create one or two statements that you can repeatedly tell your subconscious, in order to prepare it to let your feelings come up fully.

> *For example -* *"It is okay for me to remember now."*
> *For example -* *"I can handle it."*

…Write them here:

_____

_____

_____

_____

_____

_____

_____

_____

_____

_____

Re-write them on post-its now, and place them in places where you will see them often; on your car dashboard, on the bathroom mirror, and by your bed.

SECTION II

The Six Step Clearing Process

Use the six-step Clearing Process when a situation in your life seems to cause you significant upset, and your emotional response is one you have had before.

The purpose of this process is not to make you feel better, or to figure out why a situation happened, or what to do about it. We have one objective only: *to be with...*

> *to be with* your feelings in a way that is honoring and truthful and attentive

> *to be with* your emotions without blaming them on whoever 'seems' to be causing them

This kind of compassionate attention to emotions will allow them to finally dissolve. And as they dissipate your whole situation will begin to shift. Usually the entire releasing does not happen in one session. While each clearing is sufficient unto itself, it generally takes repeated sessions to bring your ego to the point of letting go of its desire to protect you from yourself.

It no longer needs to protect you. You are safe to feel now. You can heal now.

Step 1: AWARENESS AND ACCEPTANCE

Open to a heightened awareness of your uncomfortable feelings. Accept them fully.

Respond to the following questions as though you have no knowledge of the clearing process. Speak from the standpoint of being a victim.

Describe a situation you are upset about.

_____

_____

_____

_____

_____

_____

_____

Why are you upset about it?

_____

_____

_____

_____

_____

_____

_____

_____

_____

_____

_____

_____

_____

_____

_____

Be sure to keep breathing regularly as you do this inquiry. We inadvertently hold our breath to keep from feeling something painful. Conscious breathing helps the emotions come to the surface.

As you become aware of your feelings about this situation you described, be sure you are listing feelings, not what you are thinking about it all. For example, if you find yourself responding with the reasons for your feelings, that is thinking.

> E.G: "I feel so lonely" not "He didn't call again and I felt ignored."
> E.G: "I am very mad" not "I am angry because I was treated unfairly!"

We're not analyzing why the emotions are happening, or trying to do anything about them; just to become aware. This may be new for you, so have patience and take sufficient time with this step.

♥ Personal Exercises to generate deeper response

1. One catalyst for getting in touch with feelings is to repeatedly ask questions beginning with How and What. The repetition tickles the subconscious. We want to have an attitude of being curious, not knowing, exploring. The Clearing will come from getting in touch with what we don't know, not what we already know.

…What feelings are coming up in you as a result of what's happened?

_____

_____

_____

_____

_____

_____

…How intensely are you feeling?

_____

_____

_____

_____

…How would you feel if you knew this situation would never, ever change?

_____

_____

_____

_____

_____

_____

_____

_____

_____

_____

_____

2. Turn toward your feelings and fully accept them.

Lie down in a darkened room and invite your deeper mind to reveal your feelings in the face of this situation (e.g. anger).

...Write what came up here:

_____

_____

_____

_____

_____

_____

_____

_____

_____

_____

_____

_____

_____

_____

_____

_____

Then whisper to each feeling in turn, "I see you, and I accept you."

3. Use your imagination to reveal more to yourself.
 Resist the temptation to get the mind involved in "what to do" about the situation to make it better. If you start thinking about something you could do, don't do it! Instead, <u>imagine</u> doing it!

...What feelings come up in you as you imagine taking that action?

_____
_____
_____
_____
_____
_____
_____
_____
_____
_____
_____
_____
_____
_____
_____
_____
_____
_____
_____

…On a scale of 1 to 10 how fully can you accept these feelings? _____

4. The Non-Dominant Hand Exercise

This is a good technique for getting in touch with the subconscious mind. On the right of the line, write a question to yourself; e.g. 'What is happening?' using the hand you write with. On the other side, use the hand you don't write with to respond to the question in <u>cursive</u> writing - not printing.

(The effort of writing the cursive letters occupies the conscious mind, so that the ego self drops its guard that usually keeps unacceptable feelings repressed. The answers that come up may be quite revealing. Repeat asking the same question, until no further response comes up.)

Step 2: NAME YOUR FEELINGS PRECISELY

Describe them; visit them where they reside in your body.

Even though the people and circumstances are different as we repetitively play out an issue in our life, the feelings will always be exactly the same. So the doorway to healing is getting in touch with these feelings. They will lead us.

♥ Personal Exercises to generate deeper response

We want to sense for as precise a description of our emotional state as possible. The time you spend being with your feelings in order to explore and describe them is an avenue for connecting with them more intimately.

1. Find as many synonyms for the emotions that have come up as you can.

...List them here:

_____

_____

_____

_____

_____

_____

Sometimes we have developed a reaction to a situation that is habitual. That may be because it was acceptable when we were children. We now want to look under that; perhaps unearthing a deeper and more unacceptable, real feeling. We want to keep exploring what might be under the more obvious emotion.

2. As you feel complete in naming an emotion, then ask yourself, "What else? What is underneath that?"

_____

_____

_____

_____

_____

_____

_____

_____

_____

_____

_____

_____

_____

_____

_____

_____

_____

We want to stay open, knowing that we will have an intuitive feeling of 'just rightness' - like a click perhaps - when we find the exact description that fits. One good way to access that which may be beyond words is through analogy.

3. Can you describe a scene or event in nature which captures your feelings exactly?

> _...For example, "The feeling is like a being caught in the middle of a tornado." or "It feels just like a deer standing still, knowing there is a rifle trained on him."_

_____

_____

_____

_____

_____

_____

_____

_____

_____

_____

_____

_____

_____

_____

Repressed emotions are stored in every cell in the body. This is one reason why when we have physical symptoms, they are always metaphysically connected with a description of the real, deeper issue underlying them; for example, sore shoulders can represent being burdened.

The body is an out-picturing of our consciousness, so it is eager to help in the healing process. It has been waiting to be asked! Let your inner eye scan your body and see where your attention is led.

4. Where do you experience the feelings in your body?

_____

_____

_____

_____

_____

_____

_____

_____

_____

_____

_____

_____

_____

5. Take several deep breaths into that area of your body.

6. Allow your imagination to assist you in empathetically listening. After all, the imagination is being led by your subconscious, which knows what is happening. Imagine that you are looking at the body sensation in you that represents the feeling. Pretend that your inner eyes and ears are actually right there inside your body observing.

This kind of attending to something allows you to by-pass the ego-intellectual mind which has been trained to keep these feelings unconscious.

Let your imagination provide the answers and record them here:

> ...How big an area does the body sensation fill?

_____

_____

_____

_____

> ...What color is it?

_____

_____

...Is it heavy or light?

_____

_____

...Is it hard like concrete, or soft like a marshmallow?

_____

_____

...Is it warm or cool to the touch?

_____

_____

...If it had a face, what would its mouth look like?

_____

_____

_____

...Ask it why it is there, or what it wants from you.
If you could hear it talk, what would that mouth respond?

_____

_____

_____

_____

_____

_____

These kinds of questions develop a relationship and an intimacy with the feelings, and allow them to inform you. As you let yourself _be with_ them, they begin to become more acceptable to you, in and of themselves, without being attached to the situation that seemed to be the cause of them.

Step 3: ASK YOURSELF WHEN

When in the past have you felt exactly the same way?

Spirit is always supporting us! One way is by leading us to dislodge any stucknesses of the past, so we can go on in life, and live our joy; our potential! It invites us to unconsciously create repeated opportunities to clear any unfinished emotions that our psychic energy is being tied up repressing.

Therefore, when we intensely go into our feelings (as in steps 1 and 2) we will always find that we have experienced exactly the same reactions with other significant people in our life over the years.

We don't want to fall into the trap, which is very common, of believing that our reactions are unique to this situation. Yes, the circumstances were different each time - different faces; different places. However what is the same is how we felt, and perhaps what we told ourselves in the situations each time.

Can you remember another time when you felt these exact feelings?

_____

_____

_____

_____

_____

_____

_____

_____

_____

_____

_____

_____

_____

♥ Personal Exercises to generate deeper response

One very helpful technique for breaking the belief that it is THIS situation causing your feelings is to make it generic. Instead of thinking of the specific person who is involved, use the word "someone."

For example, "Someone is using me."
Or "Someone has often lied to me and I still opened myself to believing them."
Or "I depended on someone and they let me down."

1. Write your thoughts about this situation using the word 'someone' instead of the involved person's name.

_____

_____

_____

_____

_____

_____

_____

_____

_____

_____

_____

_____

2. As you are able to get in touch with other times in your life when someone brought up the same reactions in you, go back to earlier ages. Describe each situation if you can:

...As an adult -

_____

_____

_____

...As a young adult -

...In high school -

...As a child -

3. If you have access to them, get out photos of yourself, your parents, and your home when you were young, to jog your memory.

...As you look these over, see if you can imagine other times when you might have felt this same constellation of emotions as a young child -

_____

_____

_____

_____

_____

_____

_____

_____

The earliest time always turns out to have been with our parents or other caregivers when we were little - even if we can't remember it yet. We didn't even have the words or the concepts then to recognize that we were feeling, but we knew on a deep level.

And we repressed our feelings because we also knew that we had to love our parents and be loved by them in order to survive, so we could not allow ourselves to tell the truth about the anger or despair or whatever was justifiably happening within us.

And as these situations recurred again and again in our life, we didn't recognize they were the same ones happening again!

4. What is your earliest memory of feeling like this? Give as detailed a description of the situation as you can.

_____

_____

_____

_____

Step 4: OWN YOUR LIFE!

Refuse to believe that anyone or anything outside of your self is causing how you feel now.

We are socialized to believe that cause is outside of us. For example, talking with friends will usually generate lots of agreement that we are right to feel the way we do, considering the situation.

Actually, it's only our perception that makes life seem that way. In reality, we each have a unique feeling vibration and then draw to us what matches it. All people, places and things in our life are there in response to our unique frequency.

Life is a spiritual process - the inner unfolds into generating the outer. Our point of power is only through changing the within - our own vibration. The outer will change as a result - not the other way around, as most everyone believes.

The illusion is persistent, and it takes some success with shifting the inner vibration/consciousness and then seeing the cause change to make a believer out of us! However you are in that process now, and well on your way to an empowering realization of how life works.

♥ Personal Exercises to generate deeper response

Refuse to listen to your mind going over and over why he or she is to blame; why you are right in blaming them. Say "Back off!" to your mind when it returns to this theme.

1. Write an empowering statement to your mind:

For example: "Back off! It's not true that Stan's rude remark caused me to feel abused. The truth is I already had an abused feeling inside of me, and Stan's comment fed into that."

Or, "I refuse to believe that Dave's choosing not to go to church with me is why I feel so lonely. My loneliness has been waiting all these years to be felt and Dave just brought it up again!"

_____

_____

_____

_____

_____

_____

_____

_____

_____

_____

_____

_____

_____

Those we love are the people in our lives who most effectively bring up our pain. That's because they're the only ones we allow to get as close to us as our parents were.

We are divinely guided to let people into our hearts who will 'do it to us' again, so we can have the opportunity to heal.

We are the source. People show up in our lives to be pawns in our drama.

2. Write a statement of thanks to the person who seems to be causing your upset. (It is not necessary to tell them thank you directly; just do it for your own mind.)

_____

_____

_____

_____

_____

_____

_____

_____

_____

_____

_____

_____

_____

_____

_____

_____

_____

Don't kill the catalyst! Whoever seems to be causing your feelings is probably someone you care for, and overtly blaming them may detract seriously from the relationship.

Also, it's likely that your reaction to whatever they did is more intense than merited by the situation. (That is the usual indicator that our feelings are from childhood, when everything <u>was</u> very intense.)

It takes some time to really be able to disconnect your belief that a person is causing your feelings. It doesn't usually really happen until you have fully processed what's coming up in you. Meanwhile, if you want to lessen the intensity with them, it is sometimes helpful to let the person know that you are doing some inner processing work.

3. Whether or not you choose to tell it to the person involved, write a statement letting them off the hook:

For example, "Janet, I know I really reacted when you called me and cancelled last night. I just want to let you know that I've been doing some inner work and you got the benefit of it!"

Or, "Mom, thanks for letting me know how distant I've been these last few weeks. I'm doing some inner work, and when I can I'll tell you more about it."

_____
_____
_____
_____
_____
_____
_____
_____
_____
_____
_____
_____
_____
_____
_____
_____
_____
_____
_____
_____
_____
_____
_____

Step 5: BE WITH YOUR FEELINGS INTENSELY

Directly experience them.

In Steps 1 and 2 you identified and got a precise sense of the emotions coming up for you in this situation. Now we want to get to the core of the issue.

All the understanding will not dissipate the old stuck vibration. When we stop at understanding it, we are settling for the booby prize. It gives the appearance of healing, but does not accomplish the healing. We have only set the stage for healing.

Now we want to let go of understanding, analyzing or doing anything to distract from the feeling or lessen it. Return to the earliest experience of these emotions, which you already identified, and use whatever techniques are the most effective to re-experience the feelings as they felt when they were originally repressed. The exercises below offer many examples of techniques you can use to re-experience.

Say the following two statements aloud:

I allow myself to remember the details of this original memory from childhood, admitting how painful it really was. I call forth love and compassion for myself as I re-experience it.

Because I was a child, with no one to hear me, I had to repress the original feeling in order to survive the pain of it. Ever since then, it has lodged in my body and mind, like a wound, ready to come forth again when someone I love does anything to resonate it.

💗 Personal Exercises to generate deeper response

Try all of the following exercises. See which creates the most significant awareness for you.

1. Psychodrama is a very effective exercise; it has been the most powerful for me in my healing over the years.

Put an empty chair in front of you and pretend that your parent, or other original perpetrator is sitting in it. Talk to them very strongly, speaking as the voice of the child you were. Use yelling or swearing (if you can) to get in touch more vividly with your feelings.

Be very definite in telling the person what they did that hurt you and how you feel about it.

…Write some of what you said out loud here…

_____
_____
_____
_____
_____
_____
_____
_____
_____
_____
_____
_____
_____
_____
_____
_____
_____
_____
_____
_____
_____
_____

_____

_____

_____

_____

_____

_____

_____

_____

_____

_____

_____

_____

_____

_____

_____

_____

_____

_____

2. One way to remember what it was like to be a small child, with such intense feelings, is by creating opportunities to be around little ones. Go to a park with a playground, or visit friends with small children if you need to.

…What did you observe?

_____

_____

_____

_____

3. Pretend to be the little child you were, and that you are talking to a kind person who you can tell what is really happening and how you feel; a teacher or other relative perhaps. Talk in a childish voice, using words that an upset young child would use, if only someone was there to really listen to them.

…What would you say?

_____

_____

_____

_____

_____

_____

_____

_____

_____

_____

_____

_____

_____

_____

_____

_____

_____

_____

_____

_____

_____

4. Be the parent you didn't have. As the adult you now are, pretend you are holding the child self of you in your lap and listening to them tell you what they went through. Imagine that you are hugging and encouraging that little self to talk.

...What would you say as the strong, compassionate parent?

_____

_____

_____

_____

_____

_____

_____

_____

_____

_____

_____

_____

_____

_____

_____

_____

_____

_____

_____

_____

_____

_____

5. Do free-flow writing about what happened to you. Write in the first person (I) as though it were happening to you now. Don't do any punctuation or pay attention to grammar; just let it flow.

...You might start one of these phrases:

I am trying not to cry...
I wish it wasn't happening...
Could you please help me...

_____

_____

_____

_____

_____

_____

_____

_____

_____

_____

_____

_____

_____

_____

_____

_____

_____

_____

_____

6. Use the third person (she or he) approach. Tell the story of what originally happened to you by describing it as though it happened to someone else.

---

7. It is helpful for us to visualize the Spiritual Self as the witness. Let it remember both what happened to you as a child, that you needed to repress feelings about, and also the healing work you are now doing.

For example, I picture mine as perched on my right shoulder; a head nodding in approval as I do the hard parts of re-feeling trauma.

> ...Imagine: What would your Spiritual Self look like if it were to come into form, and where it might locate itself as it witnesses you?

_____

_____

_____

_____

_____

_____

_____

_____

_____

_____

8. Listen to your body. Does it feel like assuming any particular position as you again experience the difficult emotions from your childhood? For example, stretch or huddle into a ball.

> ...If so, do that. Describe the position.

_____

_____

_____

9. Let the non-intellectual parts of you assist. Let your pain express through music, art or movement; sing, draw or dance your feelings.

...Describe the non-verbal expression exercise you choose to do.

_____

_____

_____

_____

_____

_____

_____

_____

_____

10. Use the breath. Deep connected breathing, done a little more rapidly than usual, and very rhythmically, greatly facilitates the re-experiencing of emotion.

...How do you find this kind of breathing affects your clearing work?

_____

_____

_____

_____

_____

_____

_____

_____

11. Talk out loud to the Spiritual Self of the perpetrator parent. This is very effective whether the person has died, or is just not present.

It is actually more effective than if they were present with you. Remember you are not trying to change them or undo the past. Your intention is only to tell the truth to yourself of how affected you were by what happened. You would be distracted by their reaction if they were present.

It is best to imagine that they are listening attentively to you - and hearing you - for the first time.

　　　…What would you say?

_____

_____

_____

_____

_____

_____

_____

_____

_____

_____

_____

_____

_____

_____

_____

_____

_____

Step 6: LIGHTEN UP

Bring in the light of Spirit!

Only do this clearing work for short periods of time. It is very intense.

Do not be surprised if you encounter deterrents through your ego-self resisting. It might happen in the form of depression, or distractedness; catching a cold, or having headaches; being dis-oriented or irritable.

Have you had any undercurrent reactions such as these?

_____

_____

_____

_____

_____

_____

_____

_____

_____

Know that these responses are normal reactions of the ego self, which is afraid to let you in to remember that which it has had the job of repressing all these years. It is a war within the self. Your job is to stay steady and not be deterred in your intention to move ahead with feelings and dissolving this old stuff.

Realize too, that it is not your whole self involved in the re-living of the past. Only a part of you becomes re-immersed in the feelings; your real Self is being the spiritual witness.

That part of you can never be harmed by any human experience. It observes you from a space of total loving, confident in your progress on the healing path.

Can you get a sense of that part of you which witnesses and is never disturbed?

…How does that feel to you?

_____

_____

_____

_____

_____

_____

_____

_____

_____

_____

_____

_____

_____

After the clearing has occurred, you will be able to truly realize that the person or situation you identified in the beginning was not the cause of your upset.

♥ Personal Exercises to generate deeper response

1. Say the following statement aloud:

I am now willing to release _____ as the cause of these feelings in me. I see that s/he was filling in as part of my drama; as the catalyst to bring this old pain to the surface to heal it.

2. Re-visit the situation again. The feelings you will experience about it now have changed.

What is the intensity of the feelings now, from 1-10? _____

3. Describe your new awareness about the situation now.

_____

_____

_____

_____

_____

_____

_____

_____

_____

4. Say the following statement aloud:

I recognize that spiritual intelligence has guided this experience in order to facilitate my completion of the past. I am grateful! I invite the light of spiritual presence to embrace and heal me. The truth sets me free!

As this pain clears away, you will naturally open to the light that is always within.

5. How do you now feel?

_____

_____

_____

_____

_____

Clearing Process Worksheet

The Clearing Process is a power-tool! It is meant to be used anytime you are upset about something that you seem powerless to change. It's particularly indicated if your reaction to a situation has an emotional intensity greater than might be expected.

Another hint that clearing might be needed is when you find that something is happening to you again!

The next page is a worksheet that walks you through the actual Clearing Process. Make 20 copies to start with, so that you have blanks readily available when you need them.

At first they will take some time to complete. Quite soon they will become easier and eventually, after some success in using the process, you will be able to make the transition from appearance to reality mentally.

You will have internalized your awareness of how life works and become ready to live it from your seat of power; i.e. owning your own life.

Clearing Process Worksheet

Date _____

1. Who is the person (X) _____ or what is the situation I am upset about?

2. Why am I upset about it? *(Breathe)*

3. How do I feel because of what happened? *(Breathe)*

4. Where do I experience these feelings in my body?

   What is the degree of intensity of this feeling - from 1 low to 10 highest? _____

5. I am willing to fully accept my feelings, just as they are. □ Done

---

Take several deep breaths into that area of your body while you let yourself remember what happened. Feel it as intensely as possible. Even exaggerate the pain you are feeling. □ Done

---

6. When did I feel these exact same feelings in my life before? *(Breathe)*

7. What is my earliest memory of feeling like this? *(Breathe)*

8. I allow myself to remember the details of this original memory from childhood, admitting how painful it really was. I call forth compassion for myself as I re-experience it. □ Done

---

Because I was a child, with no one to hear me, I had to repress the original feeling in order to survive the pain of it. Ever since then, it has been lodged in my body and mind, like a wound, ready to come forth again when someone I love does anything to resonate it.

---

9. I now am willing to release (X) _____ as cause of these feelings in me. I see that s/he was being part of my drama, as the catalyst to bring this old pain to the surface to heal it. □ Done

---

My repressed emotion was a psychic megaphone, drawing this situation to me for healing.

---

10. I re-visit the situation (#1 above) again, but without blaming (X) for it. As I let myself be with the feelings now, they change. What is the degree of intensity of this feeling now? ___

11. The new awareness emerging in me is:

I recognize that spiritual intelligence has guided this experience in order to facilitate my completion of the past. I am grateful! I invite the light of spiritual presence to embrace and heal me. The truth sets me free!

Let the Light Continue to Shine Out of You

I love the thought: Spirit creates things by becoming them! We are all light centers. Every element of this creation is a carrier of the One Light that is creation itself. As we clear the heaviness of closed doors within us, that light is naturally let out, shining into other lives and connecting with Itself everywhere! And the vibration of all us is lifted.

This work you have completed has cleared barriers to freely Being. Each moment of life is another form of love, and the less wounding we carry, the more we can accept this enlightened way of Being. In your clarity, you become a vessel of blessing to others. You also get to have the joy and power of being fully present to your life!

Continue to do the worksheets. When I discovered the truth that my negative emotional reactions to life sourced in me, rather than in what others were doing to me, I first was shocked; then delighted; then grateful. I finally had a way to really make a significant change in my world!

It was just intellectual awareness in the beginning. Only by continuing to correct my assumptions of others' power over me was I able to internalize my understanding. The worksheet is the tool that gives you that shift.

As you continue to use clearing, you are learning healthy self-therapy. Each time you do it, it gets easier and heals more quickly. Eventually will be able to do clearing right in the moment of an interaction with a loved one. You will naturally do the process within yourself. You will get to a point where just consciously becoming aware of an old emotional reaction to someone in your present experience is enough to dissolve the toxic psychic energy further.

The deep emotional burdens you didn't even know you were carrying will be gradually dissipated. You will experience wonderful lightness of being.

I suggest that you calendar a date to re-read this workbook and all of your responses a year from now to see how much has cleared for you. You will be amazed!

If you would like to do one-on-one work with this process, please contact the author through the website or simply email clearingprocess@icloud.com. I work with many people online, where we can see each other and process effectively together and the experience is very powerful.

This Clearing Process Workbook…for Conscious Living was written with you always in mind. You came into this life and encountered challenges - maybe worse than others; maybe not. Your life journey set the stage for your clearing. You have been provided with neither too little nor too much friction, but just the right amount.

Let us know together that the healing you have done, and will do, is perfect! You have shown up for it! Congratulations!

Rev. Pat Palmer
December 31, 2012

Printed in Great Britain
by Amazon